MANTRAS FOR THE SOUL

MANTRAS FOR THE SOUL

I am powerful and
ready to take on
the world.

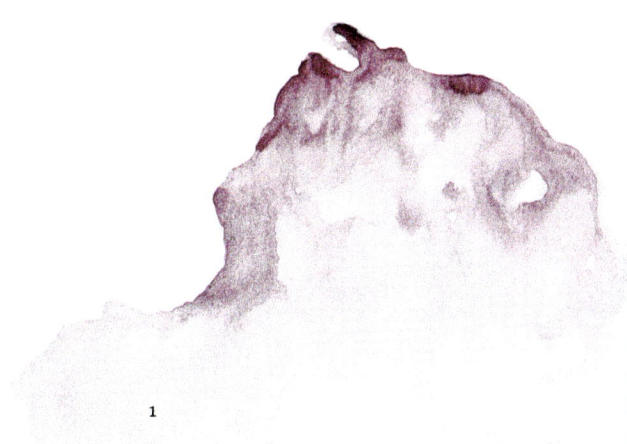

All I have is here and now,
let's do this.

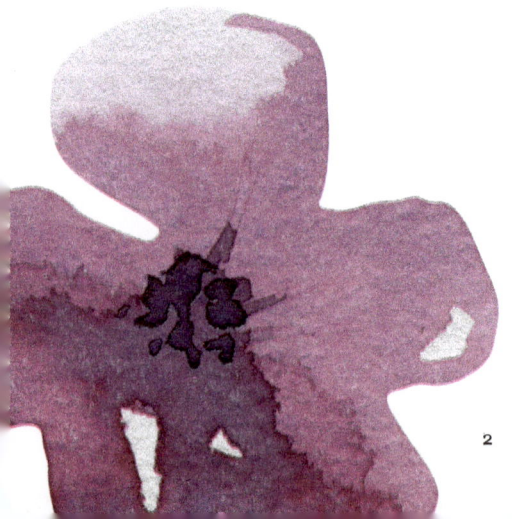

MANTRAS FOR THE SOUL

I seek what sets
my soul aflame.

Actually, I can, and I will.

I am who I am, not the person
they told me to be.

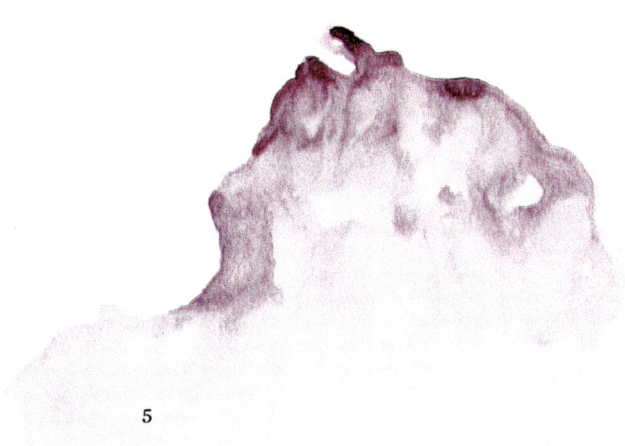

I was born to be authentic.

Mood: hell yeah!

It's a good day to be at peace.

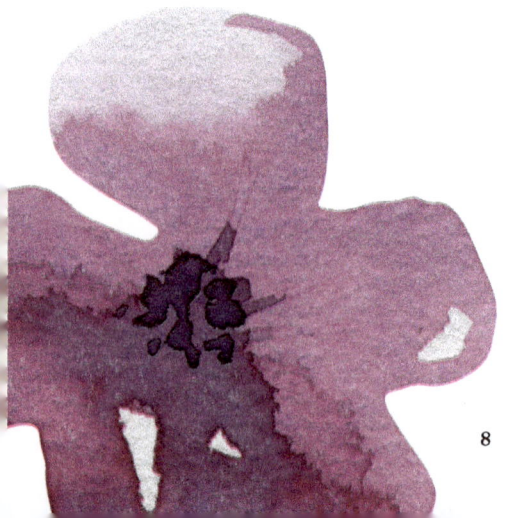

I am more than enough,
I'm overflowing!

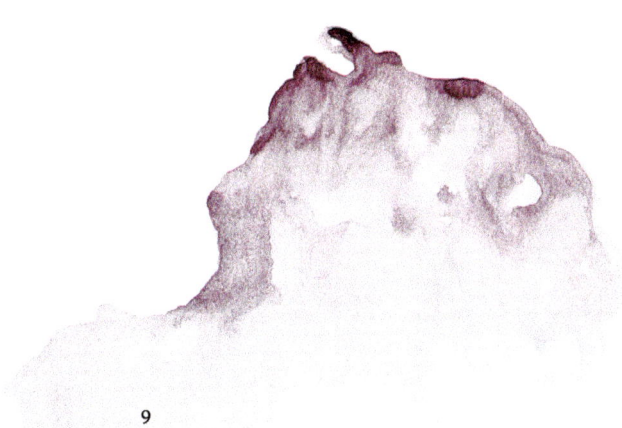

I'm a force of nature.

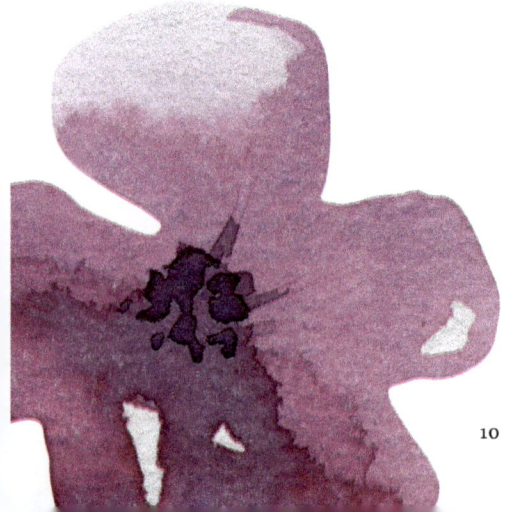

I can always be courageous.

Life can't vibe check me if
I vibe check it first.

I'm playing life on legendary.

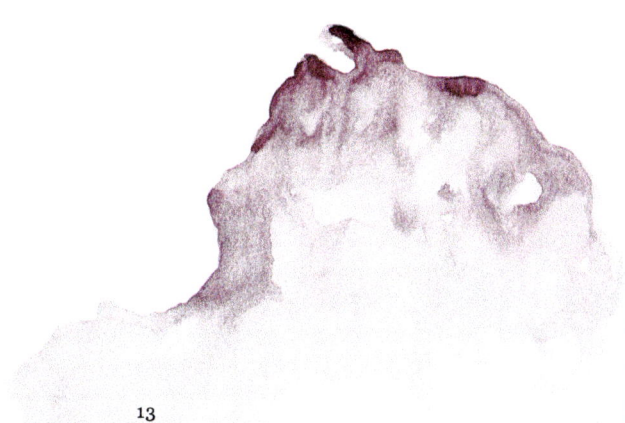

Life is tough. But so am I.

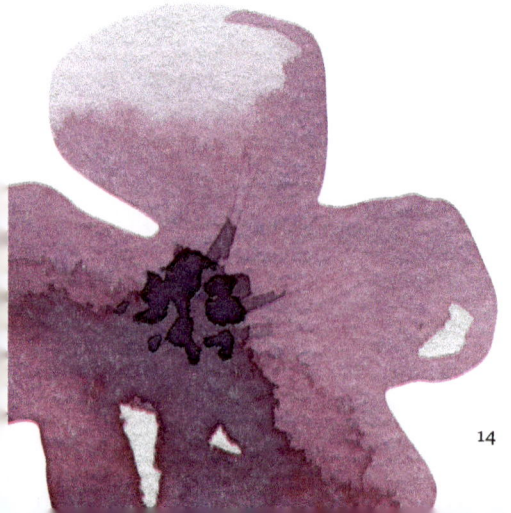

I decided to try a new trend where
I live without regrets.

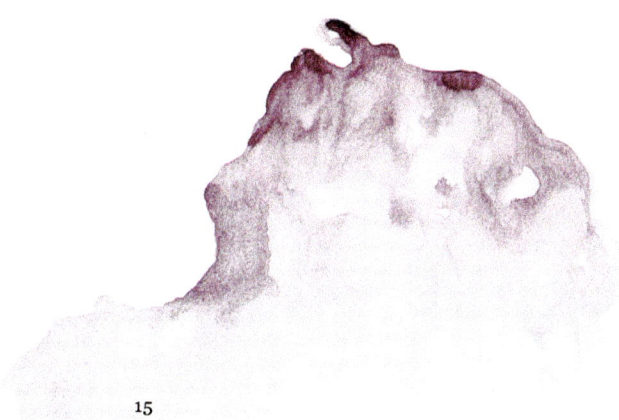

I am in the way the sun feels
after weeks of rain.

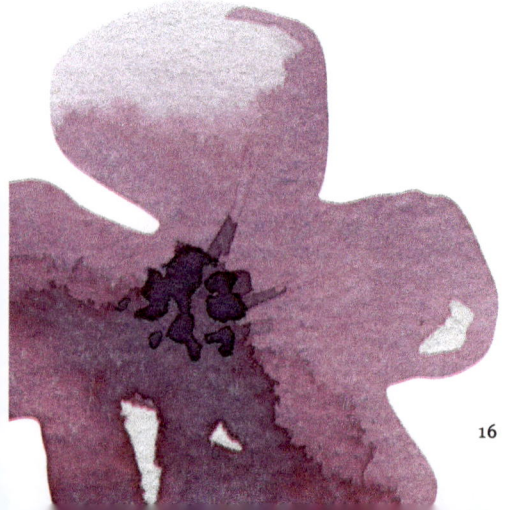

I don't have attitudes,
I have standards.

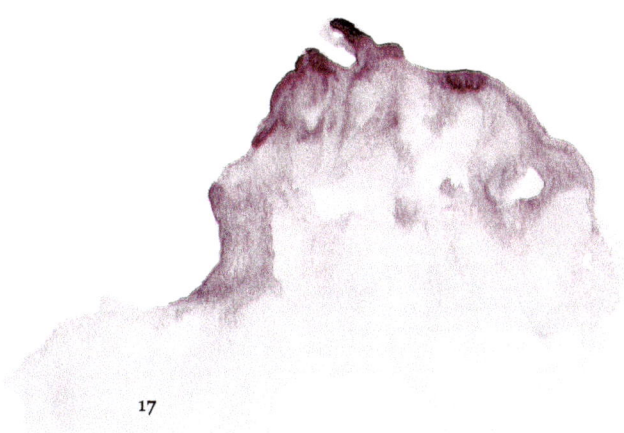

Life is too short to be anything but a legend.

I am not my experiences, but what I learned
from them.

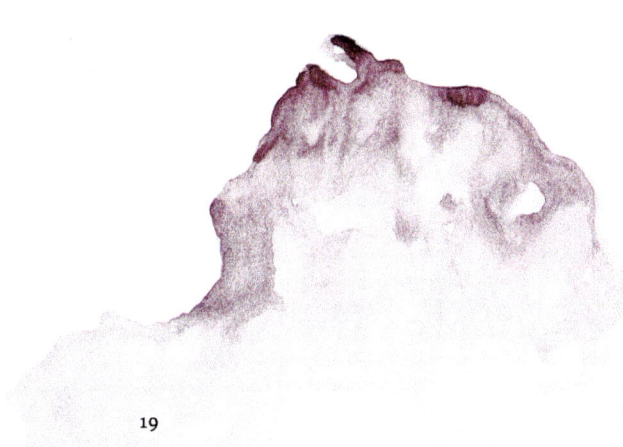

I am constantly growing and evolving, and that is the beauty of it.

I will get out there and I will do
what I'm meant to do.

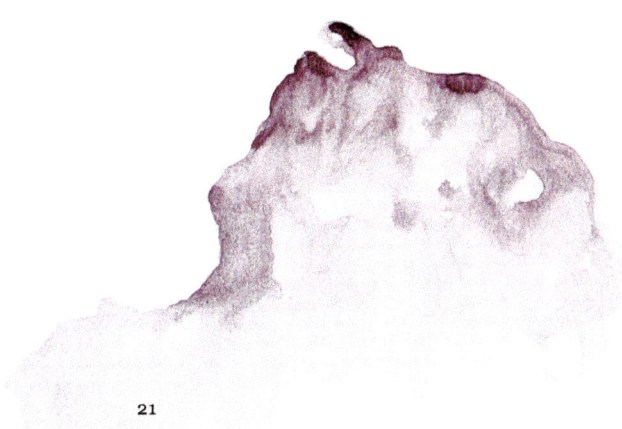

I am focused, persistent, and
ready to make a difference.

It's time to rise and grind.

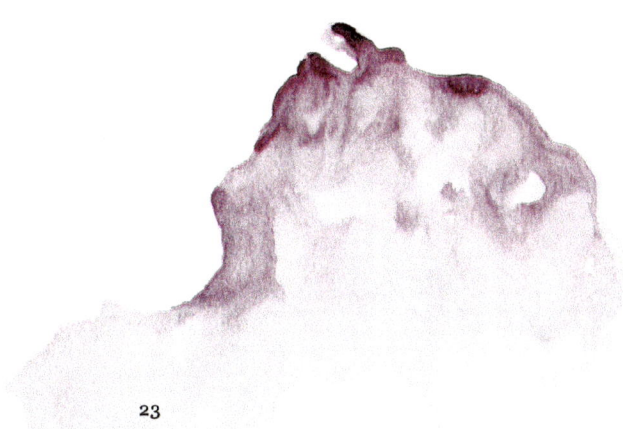

I can and will do the thing.

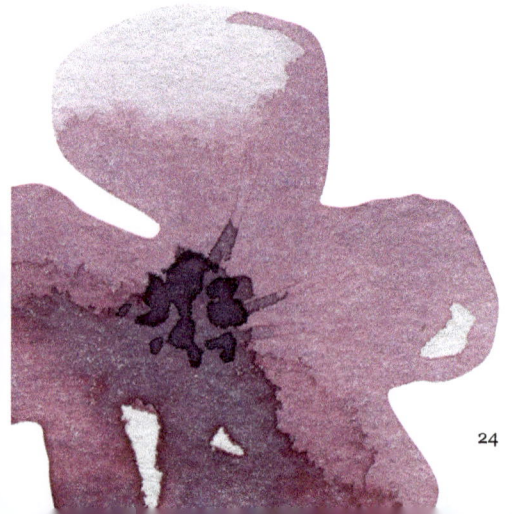

I'm my own superhero.

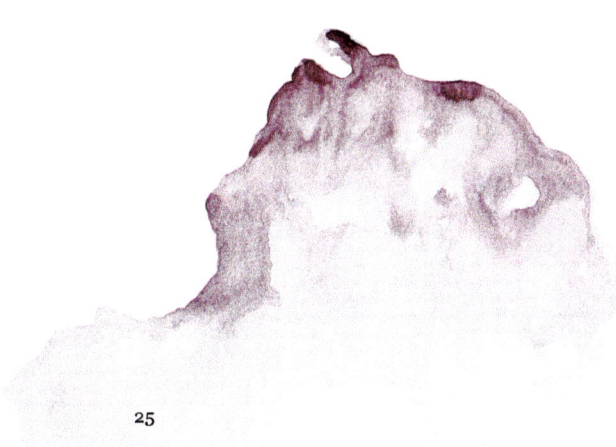

I will remember the little things that make me
happy, like warmth and hot chocolate.

My flaws are my superpower.

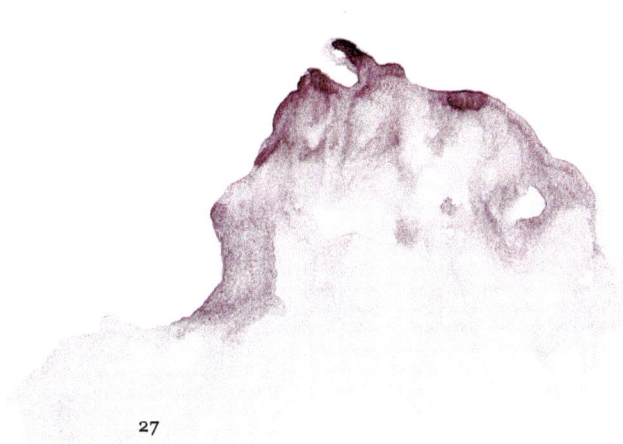

I will get it done.
I will succeed.
I will overcome.

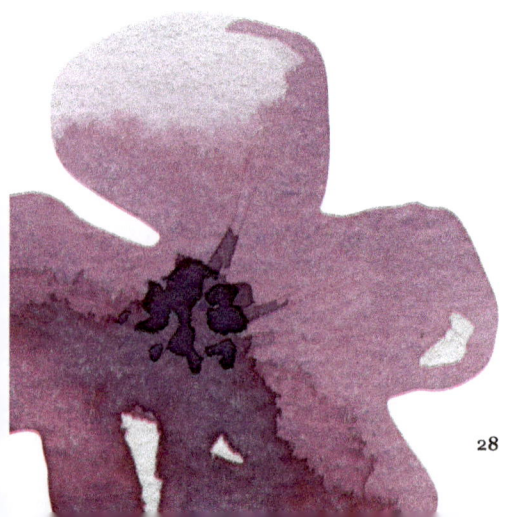

I am confident and happy with my decisions.

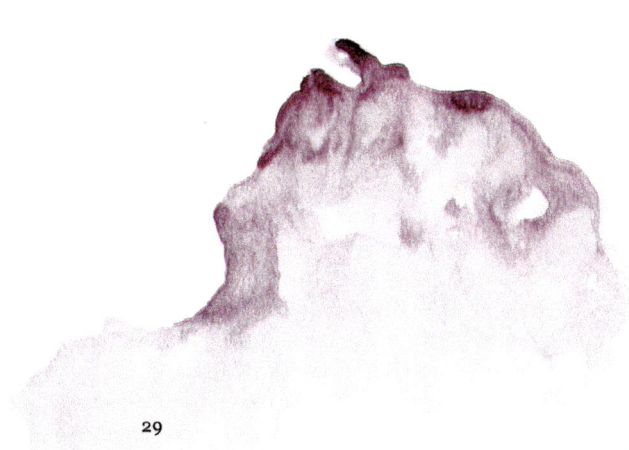

MANTRAS FOR THE SOUL

I will slow down and allow myself to breathe.

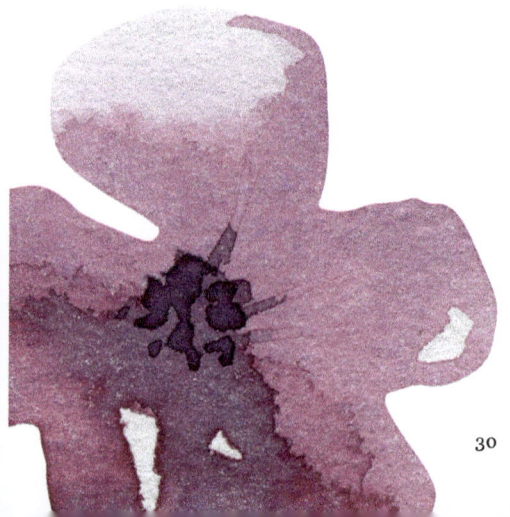

I will always persevere.

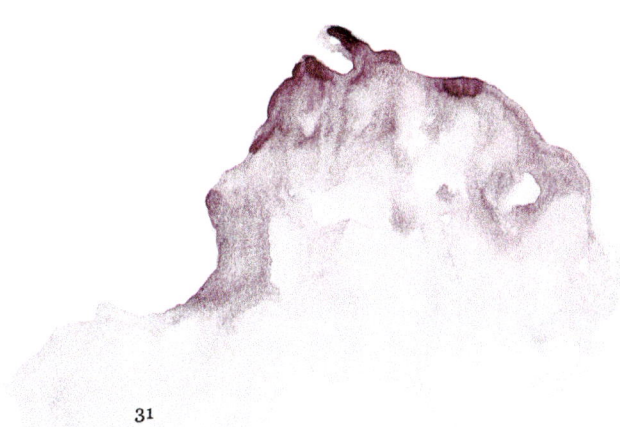

It's okay to let it go.

I will let myself breathe and feel.

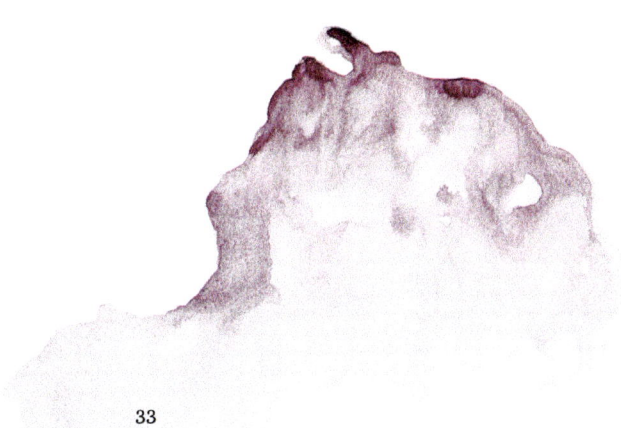

I am strong and capable.

I will always do what I need to do.

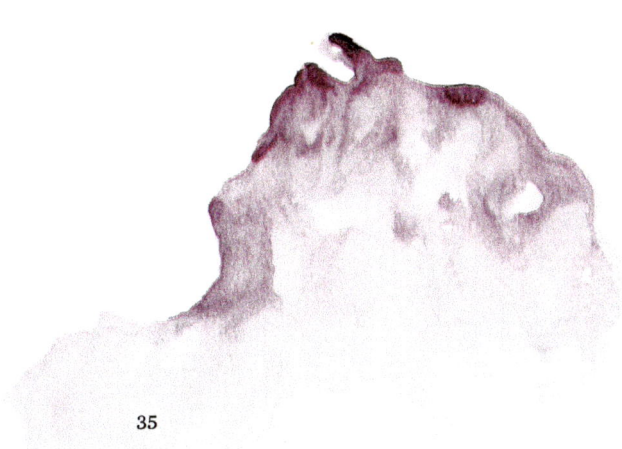

I give myself permission
to be my best self.

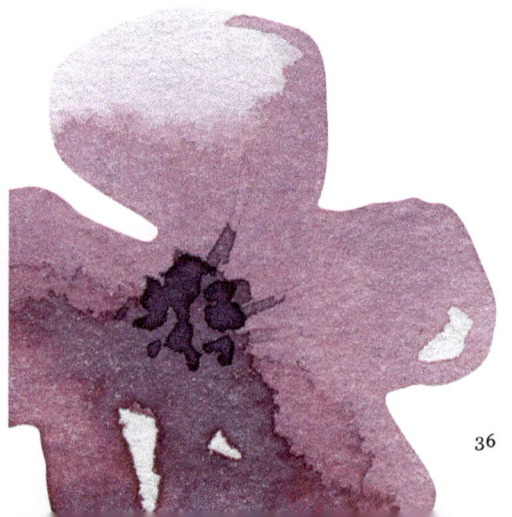

I deserve every bit of happiness.

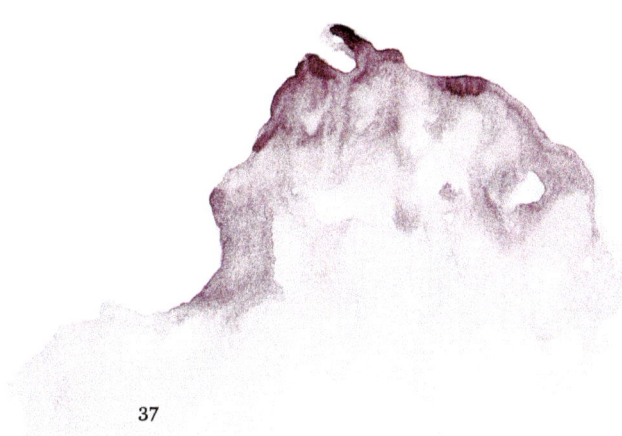

MANTRAS FOR THE SOUL

I will speak highly of myself.

I am meant to succeed, so I will.

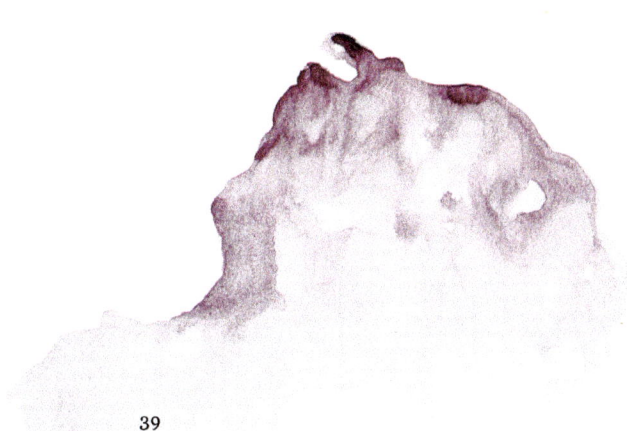

I am destined for greatness.

I am in control of who I become.

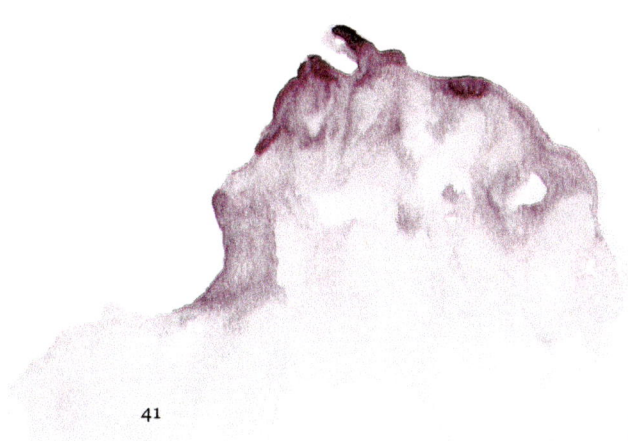

I am validated and strong.

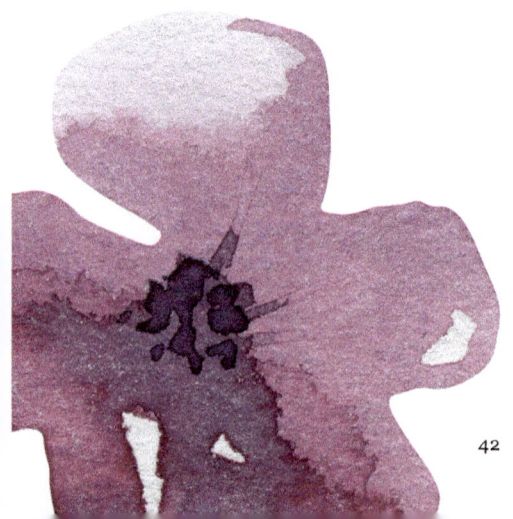

It's okay to look out for myself.

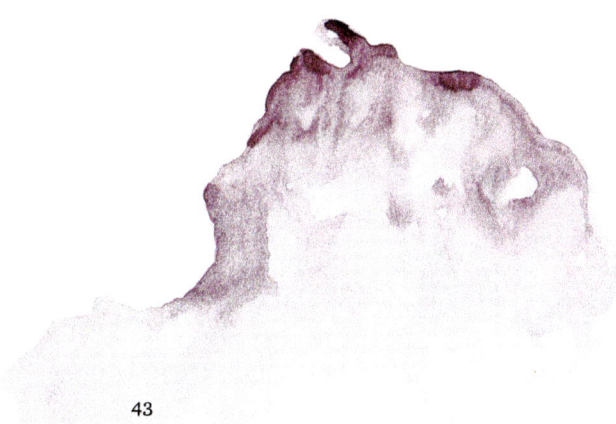

Every day, I become more confident,
loving, and powerful.

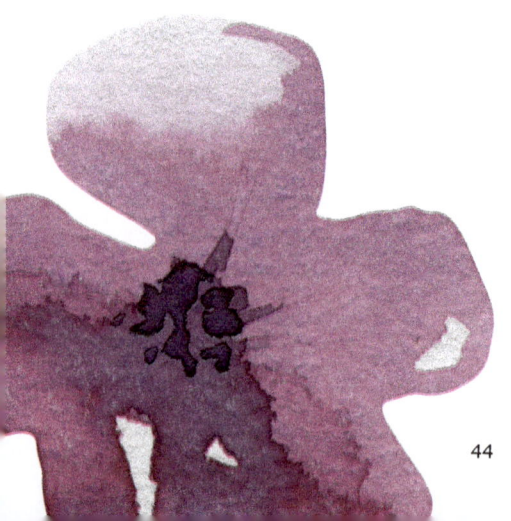

I am powerful and impressive.

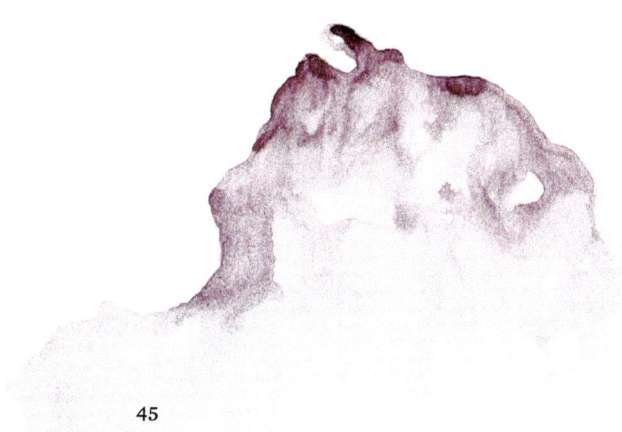

I trust myself to make the right call.

I am who I choose to be.

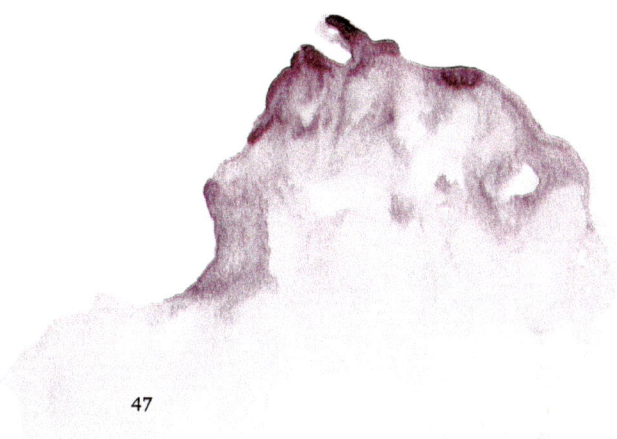

I am in control of my future.

www.ingramcontent.com/pod-product-compliance
Lightning Source LLC
Chambersburg PA
CBHW061732070526
44583CB00024B/3103